BLIND DATE
and THE ACTOR

BY HORTON FOOTE

★

★

DRAMATISTS
PLAY SERVICE
INC.

CONTENTS

BLIND DATE 5

THE ACTOR 27

BLIND DATE

BLIND DATE was originally produced by HB Playwrights Foundation Workshop Series.

BLIND DATE was presented as part of The Ensemble Studio Theatre's Marathon '86 (Curt Dempster, Artistic Director) in New York City in May 1986. It was directed by Curt Dempster; the assistant director was Richard Lichte; the set design was by Daniel Proett; the lighting design by Greg MacPherson; the costume design was by Deborah Shaw; the sound design was by Bruce Ellman; the production stage manager was Pamela Edington; and the stage manager was Jane Sanders. The cast was as follows:

ROBERT .... James Rebhorn
SARAH NANCY .... Kelly Wolf
DOLORES .... Deborah Hedwall
FELIX .... Corey Parker

CHARACTERS

ROBERT
SARAH NANCY
DOLORES
FELIX

BLIND DATE

The living room of Robert and Dolores Henry. It is empty. Robert comes in. He is a lawyer and has a briefcase, several newspapers, a package of purchases from the drugstore. He drops all these on the sofa, takes his coat off, throwing that over a chair. He calls: "Dolores." There is no answer. He kicks his shoes off and calls: "Children." Again no answer. He goes to the radio and turns it on. He gets one of the newspapers and spreads it around the room as he looks through it. He calls again: "Dolores, I am home." A voice calls back: "She's not here."

ROBERT. *(Calling.)* Where is she?

SARAH NANCY. Yes.

ROBERT. Where?

SARAH NANCY. She took the children to a friend's to spend the night.

ROBERT. Where are you?

SARAH NANCY. In my room.

ROBERT. Did your aunt say when we were having supper?

SARAH NANCY. We've had supper. We ate with the children.

ROBERT. What did you have?

SARAH NANCY. Peanut butter and jelly sandwiches. *(He is depressed by that. He goes to the window and looks out. He goes to the radio and turns it off. He sees two college yearbooks on a table. He goes and picks them up to look at them when his wife Dolores comes in.)*

ROBERT. Where is my supper?

DOLORES. What?

ROBERT. Where is my supper? Do you know what time it is? I'm starved. I have been here at least half an hour.

DOLORES. Have you forgotten our conversation at breakfast?

ROBERT. What conversation?

DOLORES. Oh, Robert. I told you to eat uptown tonight.

ROBERT. I don't remember that.

DOLORES. I told you I was not going to fix supper tonight.

ROBERT. I don't remember a single word of that.

DOLORES. You were looking right at me when I told you. I said I was giving the children peanut butter and jelly sandwiches at five-thirty and at six-thirty after their baths I was taking them over to Hannah's to spend the night so they would not be running in and out of here while Sarah Nancy was entertaining her date.

ROBERT. Does Sarah Nancy have another date?

DOLORES. Yes. Thank God. I told you that too this morning.

ROBERT. If you did, I don't remember.

DOLORES. Of course not. You never listen to a word I say. Oh, if I live through this I'll live through anything. *(Whispering.)* Don't you remember my telling you this morning that at last I had arranged another date for her? After trying desperately for three days?

ROBERT. No.

DOLORES. Well, I did. And I hope this one turns out better than the last time. I talked to Sister late this afternoon. She is just beside herself. You know, "Suppose," she said, "she takes it into her head to insult this date too." "Sister," I said, "I refuse to get discouraged. I did not get on the beauty pages of the University of Texas and the Texas A & M yearbooks on my looks alone. It was on my personality. And that can be acquired." Don't you agree?

ROBERT. I guess.

DOLORES. I wasn't born a conversationalist, you know. I can remember being as shy as the next one, but I gritted my teeth and forced myself to converse, and so can Sarah Nancy. Don't you agree?

ROBERT. I guess. Who did you get her a date with?

DOLORES. Felix.

ROBERT. Felix who?

DOLORES. Felix Robertson.

ROBERT. Is that the best you could do? My God.

DOLORES. My God, yourself. I have been calling all over town all week trying to arrange dates for the poor little thing, and you know very well I had absolutely no luck. Not a one wanted to come over here until I called Felix Robertson. I finally called Sister two days ago I was so depressed and had a frank talk with her. I explained the situation to her and she said it was nothing new. She said every time a boy has come around they don't stay long, because Sarah Nancy either won't talk or is very sarcastic. She wants me to have a frank talk with her before Felix gets here and try and help her improve her disposition and I said I would. But it's not so easy

10

to do, you know. I have been worrying over how to talk to her about all this all afternoon. And I almost have a sick headache.

ROBERT. What about supper?

DOLORES. What about your supper? What about it?

ROBERT. I forgot about eating uptown and I'm tired and I don't want to go back out. Is there anything to eat in the kitchen?

DOLORES. My God, Robert. I don't know what's in the kitchen. I feel this is a crisis in my niece's life and I really haven't had time to worry about what is in the kitchen. *(A pause.)* And don't start pouting, Robert.

ROBERT. I'm not pouting.

DOLORES. Yes, you are. I know you very well.

ROBERT. Well, my God, how much longer is this going on? Ever since your niece has been here, all you've done is worry about her.

DOLORES. I tried to explain to you. *(She looks at the room.)* Oh, look at this room. I spent all afternoon cleaning it. *(She starts to pick up his shoes, his coat, etc.)*

ROBERT. I'll do that.

DOLORES. Just take them all out. I need to be alone now with Sarah Nancy. *(He goes. She fixes pillows on the couch, rearranges a few chairs about the room, all the while singing in a bright, happy manner. After a moment she calls: "Sarah Nancy." She gets no answer and she calls again: "Sarah Nancy, Sarah Nancy, I don't want to hurry you, but it's almost time for your date to be here." Again, no response from Sarah Nancy and she is about to leave the room when Sarah Nancy appears. She is as doleful-looking as Dolores Henry is cheerful. Dolores gives her a bright, determined smile, which Sarah Nancy does not return.)* Well, you do look sweet. Is that a new dress?

SARAH NANCY. Oh, no.

DOLORES. Well, it's new to me. It's very becoming. It has a lot of style. That's what I always look for first in my clothes, style. *(Sarah Nancy gives no reaction.)* Now, precious lamb, let me tell you a little bit about the young man who is coming to see you tonight. I don't know whether you remember meeting him or not, but he says he met you at Louise Davis' swim party as you were the only one that didn't want to swim. He is Felix Robertson. *(Sarah Nancy groans.)* What's the matter, dear? Do you remember him?

SARAH NANCY. I remember him.

DOLORES. That's nice. He felt sure you would. Why do you remember him?

SARAH NANCY. Because he kept slapping me on the back and

asking me how I was.

DOLORES. He is a very sensitive boy. He was just trying to make you feel at home. And he is, as I'm sure you could tell, from a lovely family. His mother and your dear mother were girlhood friends. Now, difficult as it is for me to do, I feel I have to discuss a few things with you, Sarah Nancy, before Felix arrives. I think, dear, you have to learn to be a little more gracious to the young men that come to see you. Now, I am extremely puzzled why my phone hasn't been rung off the wall since you've been my guest, but I think last night I was given a clue. Sam and Ned, those two boys that called last week, told their mother you were extremely hard to converse with. Boys, you know, need someone peppy to talk to. *(Sarah Nancy rolls her eyes.)* Now, don't roll your eyes, darling. You know I have your best interests at heart. I want you to be just as popular as any girl here. But to accomplish that you have to learn to converse.

SARAH NANCY. I don't know what to talk about.

DOLORES. I know. I know. I called up your mother this very morning and told her all this, and she said that always seemed to be your trouble. When boys come around, you can't think of things to say. *(She goes to desk and opens a drawer and takes out a list.)* So I sat down and made a list of topics to talk about. And I thought before Felix got here, you and I could go over it, and you could memorize them and then you would always be sure of making conversation. All right, dear? *(Sarah Nancy doesn't answer. Robert enters.)*

ROBERT. Excuse me.

DOLORES. Robert?

ROBERT. How much longer are you going to be?

DOLORES. Why?

ROBERT. Because I am starving, that's why.

DOLORES. Did you look in the icebox?

ROBERT. I looked in the icebox.

DOLORES. Well …

ROBERT. The ice has all melted.

DOLORES. Well, maybe you had better ride over to the icehouse and get a block of ice.

ROBERT. I will after I've eaten. I'm hungry.

DOLORES. All right. Just be patient. I won't be long with Sarah Nancy.

ROBERT. Honey, I'm starved.

DOLORES. I know you are starved. You have told us that a thousand times. Honestly, I'm not deaf. And I'll be out there as soon as

I can, but Felix will be here any minute and Sarah Nancy and I have to go over some things first. Now excuse us, please. *(He goes.)* Now where were we? Oh, yes. I was going over my list of things to talk about. *(Dolores picks up her list and begins reading.)* One: Who is going to win the football game next Friday? Two: Do you think we have had enough rain for the cotton yet? Three: I hear you were a football player in high school. What position did you play? Do you miss football? Four: I hear you are an insurance salesman. What kind of insurance do you sell? Five: What is the best car on the market today, do you think? Six: What church do you belong to? Seven: Do you enjoy dancing? Eight: Do you enjoy bridge? *(She puts the list down.)* All right, that will do for a start. Now, let's practice. I'll be Felix. Now. Hello, Sarah Nancy. *(A pause, Sarah Nancy looks at her like she thinks she's crazy.)* Now, what do you say, Sarah Nancy?

SARAH NANCY. About what?

DOLORES. About what? About what you say when someone says hello to you, Sarah Nancy. Now, let's start again. Hello, Sarah Nancy.

SARAH NANCY. Hello.

DOLORES. Honey, don't just say hello and above all don't scowl and say hello. Smile. Hello, how very nice to see you. Let me feel your warmth. Now, will you remember that? Of course you will. All right, let's start on our questions. Begin with your first question. *(A pause.)* I'm waiting, honey.

SARAH NANCY. I forget.

DOLORES. Well, don't be discouraged. I'll go over the list carefully and slowly again. One: Who is going to win the football game next Friday? Two: Do you think we have enough rain for the cotton yet? Three: I hear you were a football player in high school. What position did you play? Do you miss football? Four: I hear you are an insurance salesman. What kind of insurance do you sell? Five: What is the best car out on the market today, do you think? Six: What church do you belong to? Seven: Do you enjoy dancing? Eight: Do you enjoy bridge? Now, we won't be rigid about the questions, of course. You can ask the last question first if you want to.

SARAH NANCY. What's the last question again?

DOLORES. Do you enjoy bridge?

SARAH NANCY. I hate bridge.

DOLORES. Well, then, sweetness, just substitute another question. Say, do you enjoy dancing?

SARAH NANCY. I hate dancing.

DOLORES. Now, you don't hate dancing. You couldn't hate

dancing. It is in your blood. Your mother and daddy are both beautiful dancers. You just need to practice is all. Now …

SARAH NANCY. Why didn't you get me a date with Arch Leon? I think he's the cute one.

DOLORES. He's going steady, honey, I explained that.

SARAH NANCY. Who is he going steady with?

DOLORES. Alberta Jackson.

SARAH NANCY. Is she cute?

DOLORES. I think she's right cute, a little common looking and acting for my taste.

SARAH NANCY. He sure is cute.

DOLORES. Well, Felix Robertson is a lovely boy.

SARAH NANCY. I think he's about as cute as a warthog.

DOLORES. Sarah Nancy.

SARAH NANCY. I think he looks just like a warthog.

DOLORES. Sarah Nancy, precious …

SARAH NANCY. That's the question I'd like to ask him. How is the hog pen, warthog?

DOLORES. Precious, precious.

SARAH NANCY. Anyway, they are all stupid.

DOLORES. Who, honey?

SARAH NANCY. Boys.

DOLORES. Precious, darling.

SARAH NANCY. Dumb and stupid. *(She starts away.)*

DOLORES. Sarah Nancy, where in the world are you going?

SARAH NANCY. I'm going to bed.

DOLORES. Sarah Nancy, what is possessing you to say a thing like that. You're just trying to tease me.

SARAH NANCY. Oh, no I'm not. *(She starts away.)*

DOLORES. Sarah Nancy, you can't go to bed. You have a young man coming to call on you at any moment. You have to be gracious …

SARAH NANCY. I don't feel like being gracious. I'm sleepy. I'm going to bed.

DOLORES. Sarah Nancy, you can't. Do you want to put me in my grave? The son of one of your mother's dearest friends will be here at any moment to call on you, and you cannot be so rude as to go to bed and refuse to receive him. Sarah Nancy, I beg you. I implore you.

SARAH NANCY. Oh, all right. *(She sits down.)* Ask me some questions.

DOLORES. No, dear. You ask me some questions.

SARAH NANCY. What church do you attend?

14

DOLORES. That's lovely. That's a lovely question to begin with. Now I'll answer as Felix will. Methodist.

SARAH NANCY. That's a dumb church.

DOLORES. Sarah Nancy.

SARAH NANCY. I think it's a dumb church. It's got no style. We used to be Methodist but we left for the Episcopal. They don't rant and rave in the Episcopal Church.

DOLORES. And they don't rant and rave in the Methodist Church either, honey. Not here. Not in Harrison.

SARAH NANCY. Last time I was there they did.

DOLORES. Well, things have changed. Anyway, you're not supposed to comment when he answers the questions, you're just supposed to sit back and listen to the answers as if you're fascinated and find it all very interesting.

SARAH NANCY. Why?

DOLORES. Because that's how you entertain young men, graciously. You make them feel you are interested in whatever they have to say.

SARAH NANCY. Suppose I'm not.

DOLORES. Well, it is not important if you are or not, you are supposed to make them think you are. *(Robert enters.)*

ROBERT. Dolores.

DOLORES. What?

ROBERT. The children are on the phone.

DOLORES. What do they want?

ROBERT. They want to talk to you.

DOLORES. Ask them what they want. Tell them I can't talk now. *(Sarah Nancy is looking at the yearbook.)*

SARAH NANCY. How did you make the beauty page at two colleges?

DOLORES. Personality. I always knew how to keep a conversation going.

ROBERT. Dolores.

DOLORES. Yes.

ROBERT. They say they won't tell me what they want. They'll only tell you.

DOLORES. All right. *(She goes.)*

SARAH NANCY. Did you go to college with Aunt Dolores?

ROBERT. We met the year she graduated.

SARAH NANCY. She was beautiful.

ROBERT. I guess she was. *(Dolores comes in.)*

DOLORES. They forgot their teddy bears. I said you would bring them over.

ROBERT. They're nine and ten years old. What do they want with teddy bears?

DOLORES. They still sleep with them. You know that.

ROBERT. Well, I'm not driving anywhere with two teddy bears for two half-grown children.

DOLORES. Why are you being so difficult?

ROBERT. I am not difficult. I am hungry and tired. I worked hard all day.

DOLORES. Well, I didn't exactly have a ball today myself, mister. If I find you something to eat, will you take those teddy bears over to the children?

ROBERT. All right. I'll be the laughingstock of the town, but I'll do it. *(She goes.)*

SARAH NANCY. How do you get on a beauty page?

ROBERT. Well, you have to be pretty to start with, I guess. I think a committee of some kind looks the girls on campus over and makes recommendations and I guess they have judges. But I really don't know. You'll have to ask your aunt that.

SARAH NANCY. How did you meet Aunt Dolores?

ROBERT. At a dance. I think. Yes, I think it was at a dance the first time I met her. And I asked her for a date and six weeks later I popped the question.

SARAH NANCY. What does that mean?

ROBERT. What?

SARAH NANCY. Popping the question.

ROBERT. You know. I asked her to marry me. *(Sarah Nancy makes a face.)* What are you making a face about?

SARAH NANCY. I don't know. I sure hope nobody pops a question to me.

ROBERT. Well, they will someday.

SARAH NANCY. Who?

ROBERT. Some boy or other.

SARAH NANCY. I don't know any boys.

ROBERT. Of course you know some boys.

SARAH NANCY. Not any I'd want to pop the question to me. *(Dolores comes in.)*

DOLORES. I opened a can of chile and a can of tamales and sliced some tomatoes. Will that do you?

ROBERT. Thanks. *(He goes.)*

16

SARAH NANCY. Any of the dumb boys I know try popping a question to me, I'll kick them in the stomach.

DOLORES. What in the world are you talking about, honey? *(The doorbell rings.)* There he is. Now, quickly, let me see how you look. *(She forces Sarah Nancy to stand up.)* Oh, pretty. *(Sarah Nancy sticks out her tongue.)* Oh, Sarah Nancy. *(Dolores goes to the door and opens it.)* Come in, Felix. *(Felix comes in.)* How handsome you look. I believe you two have met?

FELIX. Yes.

SARAH NANCY. What church do you attend?

FELIX. What?

SARAH NANCY. What church do you attend?

FELIX. Methodist.

DOLORES. *(Jumping in nervously.)* Sarah Nancy is an Episcopalian. She is very devout. Felix is very devout, too, you know.

SARAH NANCY. Who is going to win the football game on Friday?

FELIX. We are.

SARAH NANCY. Why?

FELIX. Because we are the best team.

SARAH NANCY. Who says so?

FELIX. Everybody knows that. Do you like football?

SARAH NANCY. No.

FELIX. No?

SARAH NANCY. No.

FELIX. Do you like …

SARAH NANCY. I hate sports. I like to read. Do you like to read?

FELIX. No.

DOLORES. Well, you know what they say, opposites attract. *(She laughs merrily. Felix laughs. Sarah Nancy scowls.)* Well, I'll stay and visit just a few minutes longer and then I'll leave you two young people alone. How is your sweet mother, Felix?

FELIX. OK.

DOLORES. Your mother and Sarah Nancy's mother and I were all girls together. Did your mother tell you that? My, the good times we used to have together.

FELIX. Do you have a radio?

DOLORES. Yes, over there. *(He goes to the radio and turns it on.)*

FELIX. Do you want to dance?

SARAH NANCY. No, I hate dancing. What church do you belong to?

DOLORES. You asked him that before, Sarah Nancy, honey,

remember? He said he was a Methodist and I said you were an Episcopalian …

SARAH NANCY. Oh. *(Dolores finds a way to get behind Felix and she begins mouthing a question for Sarah Nancy to ask.)* What do you do?

FELIX. What do you mean?

SARAH NANCY. For a living.

FELIX. Right now I'm in insurance. But I'm leaving that. Not enough money in it. I'm going to be a mortician.

SARAH NANCY. What's that?

DOLORES. An undertaker, honey.

SARAH NANCY. How do you get to do that?

FELIX. You go to school.

SARAH NANCY. What kind of school?

FELIX. A mortician school.

SARAH NANCY. Oh, who teaches you?

FELIX. Other morticians. *(Dolores begins to subtly mouth another question to her; Sarah Nancy continues to ignore her, so Dolores finally gives up.)*

DOLORES. I'm going now and leave you two young people alone to enjoy yourselves. *(She goes. He goes to the radio and moves the dial from one program to another.)*

FELIX. There is nothing on I want to hear. *(He turns the radio off. He sits down and looks at Sarah Nancy smiling.)* Having a good time on your visit here?

SARAH NANCY. It's okay.

FELIX. Let's play some games. What games do you like to play?

SARAH NANCY. I never played any.

FELIX. Never played any games?

SARAH NANCY. No.

FELIX. All right, I'll teach you one. How about Ghosts?

SARAH NANCY. Ghosts.

FELIX. It's the name of the game. You start a word to be spelled and the one that spells a word is a third of a ghost. Get it?

SARAH NANCY. No.

FELIX. Well, maybe it isn't too much fun with just two playing. I know, let's see who can name the most books of the Bible. I'll go first. *(He doesn't wait for her to comment and he begins to rattle off the names of the books.)* Genesis, Exodus, Leviticus … *(He closes his eyes as he thinks of them and he takes it all very seriously. Sarah Nancy stares at him as if he is insane. When he gets to Daniel she slips quietly out of the room and is gone by the time he begins the New Testament. He is not aware she is gone. Robert comes in. Felix is concentrating so hard he doesn't see him. Robert looks at him like he is crazy, shakes his head in disbelief and leaves the room. Felix is unaware of any of it. He says the names very fast as if speed were part of the game, so fast in fact that the names should not always be distinct. When he finishes, he opens his eyes.)* How did I do? I think I got every one. *(He looks at his watch.)* I did it in a pretty fair amount of time too. Now, let's see what you can do. *(He suddenly becomes aware she is not in the room. Calling:)* Sarah Nancy. *(He is puzzled by her disappearance and is about to go to the door leading into the rest of the house to call her when Robert comes in with two teddy bears.)*

ROBERT. Hello, Felix. *(They shake hands.)* What's new?

FELIX. Not a whole lot.

ROBERT. You're looking well.

FELIX. Thank you, sir. *(Robert starts out the front door.)* Excuse me. Do you know where Sarah Nancy is?

ROBERT. No, I don't, son.

FELIX. She was here a minute ago. We were having a contest to see who could name the most books of the Bible.

ROBERT. Who won?

FELIX. I don't know. She was here when I started, but when I finished and opened my eyes she was gone.

ROBERT. Just sit down and relax. She'll be back.

FELIX. Yes, sir. *(Robert goes out. Felix sits down. Dolores comes in looking stricken.)*

DOLORES. Felix, Sarah Nancy has sent me out to apologize to you and beg your forgiveness. She has been stricken, suddenly, with a very bad sick headache. She's suffered from them, she says, since childhood, and the worst of it is the poor darling never, never knows when they will strike. She says she was sitting here listening to you rattle off all the books of the Bible and having one of the liveliest times of her life, when her attack began. She is just heartbroken, the poor little thing. She slipped out not wanting to disturb you, to take an aspirin, hoping to find relief for her headache, so she could resume the lovely time she was having with you, but she got no relief from the aspirin, and she says now the only relief are cold packs on her head and total, total silence. She is quite stricken, poor sweet thing. Too stricken to even come and say good night. Whatever will Felix think of me, she said, why precious darling, I reassured her, he will most certainly understand. I know you do. Don't you?

FELIX. Oh, yes, ma'am.

DOLORES. How is your sweet mother?

FELIX. Just fine, thank you, ma'am.

DOLORES. And your daddy's well?

FELIX. Oh, yes, ma'am.

DOLORES. Tell your mother and daddy hello for me.

FELIX. I will. *(A pause.)* They said when I came over here to say hello for them.

DOLORES. Thank you. *(A pause.)*

FELIX. Well, I guess I'll be going on home.

DOLORES. All right, Felix.

FELIX. Tell Nancy Sarah …

DOLORES. Sarah Nancy.

FELIX. Oh, yes. Sarah Nancy. Tell her I hope she feels better.

DOLORES. I will.

FELIX. Tell her I said all the books in the Bible under ten minutes, and if she thinks she can beat that to call me up and I'll come over and time her.

DOLORES. I'll tell her that.

FELIX. Well, good night again.

DOLORES. Good night to you, Felix dear. *(He goes. Dolores sighs. She begins to turn the lights off when Sarah Nancy comes out.)* What are you doing out here, Sarah Nancy?

SARAH NANCY. I want to listen to the radio.

DOLORES. You cannot listen to the radio. You can be seen from the street if you sit in this room listening to the radio. I told that boy that you were mortally ill with a sick headache and you cannot appear five minutes later perfectly well and sit in the living room and listen to the radio.

SARAH NANCY. I want to hear Rudy Vallee.

DOLORES. You will not hear Rudy Vallee and run the risk of someone seeing you and telling Felix about it. What possesses you? I ask two lovely young men over last week and you refuse to speak to either of them all evening. I ask this sweet, charming boy over tonight and you walk out of the room while he is saying the books of the Bible. Well, I tell you one thing, I will not ask another single boy over here again until you decide to be gracious. And I know you can be gracious, as gracious as any girl here. Anyone with the lovely mother you have can certainly be gracious. *(Robert enters.)* Oh, you gave me such a start. I thought you were Felix. How were the children?

ROBERT. All right.

DOLORES. Did you tell them to behave themselves and to mind Hannah and to get to bed when she told them to?

ROBERT. No.

DOLORES. Why not?

ROBERT. Because it would have done no good. They were all running around like a bunch of wild Indians. They weren't any more interested in those teddy bears than I am. Did Felix pop the question to you, Sarah Nancy?

SARAH NANCY. No. And if he had, I'd have knocked his head off.

DOLORES. What's all this about popping questions?

ROBERT. I was telling Sarah Nancy how we met and after six weeks I asked you to marry me.

DOLORES. Six weeks? It was three months.

ROBERT. Six weeks.

DOLORES. I only went out twice with you in the first six weeks. We didn't start going steady until our third date. You took me to a tea dance at your frat house and you asked me to wear your fraternity pin and I said I had to think about it, as I wasn't in the habit of just casually accepting fraternity pins like some girls I knew. *(The door opens and Felix enters.)*

FELIX. Excuse me. I left my hat.

DOLORES. Oh, Felix. Isn't this remarkable. I was just about to go to the phone and call you and tell you that Sarah Nancy had completely recovered from her headache. You hadn't gone five minutes when she came out and said the aspirin worked after all and where is Felix and she was so distressed that you had gone that she insisted I go to the phone and see if you wouldn't come back which I was about to do. Isn't that so, Sarah Nancy? *(Sarah Nancy doesn't answer.)*

FELIX. Did Mrs. Henry tell you I said all the names of the Bible in under ten minutes?

DOLORES. Yes, I did. Didn't I, Sarah Nancy? *(Sarah Nancy doesn't answer.)* And she was so impressed. Weren't you, Sarah Nancy? *(Again no answer from Sarah Nancy.)*

FELIX. Want to hear me do it again? You can time me this time.

SARAH NANCY. No.

FELIX. Want to play another game then? How about Movie Stars?

DOLORES. That sounds like fun. Doesn't it, Robert? How do you play that?

FELIX. Well, you think of initials like R.V., and you all try to guess who I'm thinking of.

SARAH NANCY. Rudy Vallee.

FELIX. No, you give up?

DOLORES. I do. I never can think of anything. Can you think of who it is, Robert?

ROBERT. No.

FELIX. Do you give up, Sarah Nancy?

SARAH NANCY. No. *(A pause. There is silence:)*

FELIX. Now do you give up?

SARAH NANCY. I'll die before I give up. *(Again silence.)*

DOLORES. Honey, you can't take all night. It won't be any fun then. I think there should be a time limit, Felix, and if we don't guess it …

FELIX. *(Interrupting.)* Give up?

SARAH NANCY. No.

DOLORES. Let's have a five-minute time limit. *(She looks at her watch.)* Five minutes is almost up.

FELIX. Give up?

SARAH NANCY. No.

DOLORES. Time is up. Who is it?

FELIX. Rudolph Valentino.

DOLORES. Rudolph Valentino. Imagine. Now why couldn't I have thought of that? Isn't that a fun game, Sarah Nancy honey? Why don't you pick some initials?

SARAH NANCY. O.B.

DOLORES. O.B. My. O.B. Can you think of an O.B., Felix?

FELIX. Not yet.

DOLORES. Can you, Robert?

ROBERT. No.

DOLORES. My, you picked a hard one, Sarah honey. O.B. Can she give us a clue?

FELIX. Yes. You can ask things like is it a man or a woman.

DOLORES. Is it a man or a woman?

SARAH NANCY. A woman.

DOLORES. A woman. My goodness.

SARAH NANCY. Give up?

DOLORES. I do. Do you, Felix?

FELIX. Yes. Who is it?

SARAH NANCY. Olive Blue.

FELIX. Olive Blue. Who is she?

SARAH NANCY. A girl back home.

FELIX. She's not a movie star.

SARAH NANCY. Who said she was?

FELIX. Well, goose. They're supposed to be movie stars.

SARAH NANCY. You're a goose yourself.

DOLORES. Sarah Nancy.

SARAH NANCY. It's a dumb game anyway.

FELIX. Well, let's play Popular Songs.

DOLORES. That sounds like fun. How do you do that?

FELIX. Well, you hum or whistle part of a song and the others have to guess what it is.

DOLORES. Oh, grand. Doesn't that sound like fun, Sarah Nancy? *(Again no answer from Sarah Nancy.)* Why don't you whistle something, Sarah Nancy?

SARAH NANCY. I can't whistle.

DOLORES. Well, then hum something.

SARAH NANCY. I can't hum either.

FELIX. I'll hum and you all guess. *(He hums.)* Can you guess?

DOLORES. I can't. Can you, Robert?

ROBERT. No.

DOLORES. Can you, Sarah Nancy?

SARAH NANCY. No, but I never will be able to guess what he hums, because he can't carry a tune.

DOLORES. Well, I don't agree at all. I think Felix has a very sweet voice.

ROBERT. Then how come you can't tell what he's humming?

DOLORES. Because I didn't know the song, I suppose.

ROBERT. What was the song, Felix?

FELIX. "Missouri Waltz."

ROBERT. Don't you know the "Missouri Waltz" when you hear it?

DOLORES. Yes, I know the "Missouri Waltz" when I hear it. Hum something else, Felix. *(He hums another tune. Again very flat.)* Now what's the name of that, honey?

FELIX. "Home Sweet Home."

ROBERT. "Home Sweet Home." My God! *(Dolores glares at Robert.)*

DOLORES. Oh, of course. It was on the tip of your tongue. All right, Sarah Nancy honey, it's your turn.

FELIX. No, it's still my turn. I keep on until you guess what I'm singing.

SARAH NANCY. How are we going to guess what you're singing when you can't sing?

FELIX. I certainly can sing. I'm in the choir at the Methodist church. I'm in a quartet that sings twice a year at the Lion's Club.

SARAH NANCY. If you can sing, a screech owl can sing.

DOLORES. Sarah Nancy, honey.

SARAH NANCY. I'd rather listen to a jackass bray then you sing. You look like a warthog and you bray like a jackass.

FELIX. Who looks like a warthog?

SARAH NANCY. You do.

FELIX. I'm rubber and you're glue, everything you say bounces off of me and sticks on you.

SARAH NANCY. Warthog. You are a stinking warthog and I wish you would go on home so I could listen to Rudy Vallee in peace.

FELIX. Don't worry. I'm going home. I didn't want to come over here in the first place but my mama bribed me to come over here. Well, a million dollars couldn't make me stay here now and two million couldn't ever get me here again if you were here. *(He leaves.)*

DOLORES. Oh, my God. I have never seen such carrying on in my life. Sarah Nancy, what am I going to tell Sister? She will take to her bed when I report this. Absolutely have a breakdown.

SARAH NANCY. I'm sorry. I'm not going to lie and tell some old fool jackass they can sing when they can't.

ROBERT. I agree with Sarah Nancy. He can't carry a tune at all.

DOLORES. Nobody asked your opinion.

ROBERT. Well, I'm giving it to you whether you asked for it or not.

DOLORES. And I don't want to hear it. How can you expect Sarah Nancy to learn to be gracious if we don't set an example?

ROBERT. I didn't tell her not to be gracious. I just told her that I agreed with what she said about his singing. I'm being honest. If that's ungracious. All right. I'd rather be honest than gracious.

DOLORES. That's all right for you. You're a man. But let me tell you right now I didn't get on two beauty pages by being honest, but by being gracious to people. But I'm whipped now and worn out. I've done all I can do. I can do no more. *(She leaves.)*

ROBERT. I guess your aunt's a little upset.

SARAH NANCY. I guess so. Do you mind if I listen to Rudy Vallee on the radio?

ROBERT. No. *(She turns on the radio. She turns the dial.)*

SARAH NANCY. What time is it?

ROBERT. Almost ten.

SARAH NANCY. Shoot. I missed Rudy Vallee.

ROBERT. Well, you can hear him next week.

SARAH NANCY. I'll be home next week.

ROBERT. I'm going to go see to your aunt. Will you be all right?

SARAH NANCY. Sure. *(He goes. She gets the yearbooks. She looks at one and then the other. Felix comes in.)*

FELIX. Where's Mrs. Henry?

SARAH NANCY. I don't know.

FELIX. I told my mama what happened and she said I owed Mrs. Henry an apology for speaking like I did. I told her what you said to me and she said it didn't matter how other people acted, I had to remember that I was a gentleman and that I was always to act in a gentlemanly fashion. So tell Mrs. Henry I'm here and I want to apologize. *(She goes. He sees the yearbooks. He looks at them. Sarah Nancy comes in.)* Did you tell her?

SARAH NANCY. No. I couldn't. She's gone to bed. She has a sick headache.

FELIX. *(He points to the book.)* She was pretty, wasn't she?

SARAH NANCY. Yes, she was.

FELIX. You don't sing any better than I do.

SARAH NANCY. I didn't say I did.

FELIX. And you're never going to be on any beauty pages, I bet.

SARAH NANCY. I didn't say I would.

FELIX. Don't you care?

SARAH NANCY. No. *(There is silence. An uncomfortable silence. He closes the yearbook.)*

FELIX. I can't think of a whole lot to talk about. Can you?

SARAH NANCY. No.

FELIX. Your aunt is quite a conversationalist. It's easy to talk when she's around.

SARAH NANCY. I guess. *(A pause. Silence.)*

FELIX. Do you mind if I stay on here for a while?

SARAH NANCY. No.

FELIX. I told my mother I'd stay at least another hour. If you get sleepy, you just go on to bed. I'll just sit here and look at these yearbooks.

SARAH NANCY. I'm not sleepy.

FELIX. You want one of the yearbooks?

SARAH NANCY. Thank you. *(He hands her one. She opens it. He takes one and opens it. After a beat they are both completely absorbed in looking at the yearbooks. They continue looking at them as the light fades.)*

End of Play

PROPERTY LIST

Sofa
Chairs
Radio
Table
2 yearbooks
Pillows
Desk
List (in desk drawer)
Briefcase
Newspapers
Package
2 teddy bears

SOUND EFFECTS

Radio
Doorbell

THE ACTOR

The world premiere of THE ACTOR was presented at the Royal National Theatre in London on July 12, 2002. It was directed by Colin Snell. The cast was as follows:

HORACE .... Ben Hynes
HORACE, SR. .... Michael Stacey
DOROTHY .... Olivia Brown
JIM .... Ben Smith
ELIZABETH .... Laura Derkins

CHARACTERS

HORACE
HORACE, SR.
GIRLS
BOY
1ST BOY
2ND BOY
DOROTHY
JIM
ELIZABETH

SETTING

Early spring, 1932.

THE ACTOR

A section of a hall in the Harrison high school. Horace Robedaux, Jr., 15, is there. He looks at his wristwatch, he hums to himself several bars of "Brother, Can You Spare a Dime," looks up and down the hallway and then begins to sing to himself snatches of "Brother, Can You Spare a Dime."

HORACE. *(Singing.)*
   "Once I built a railroad,
   Made it run,
   Made it race against time.
   Once I built a railroad,
   Now it's done,
   Brother, can you spare a dime?"
(Two boys, a year or so older than Horace, come down the hall, each with a girl. They carry schoolbooks.)
GIRLS. Hello, Horace.
HORACE. Hi.
1ST BOY. Hi, Horace.
HORACE. Hi.
2ND BOY. Rudolph Valentino, what's new?
HORACE. Not much. *(They walk down the hall. Horace talks to the audience as to a close friend.)* I hate it when somebody calls me Rudolph Valentino. I was walking in front of Rugeley's Drugstore yesterday on the way to the post office when old blowhard Mayor Armstrong came out of the drugstore and called out in a loud voice, "Hey there, Valentino," and all the old men sitting in front of the drugstore laughed like it was the funniest thing they had ever heard. I didn't think it was funny at all, but I pretended like I did and I just said, "Pretty well, thank you, Mr. Mayor" and walked on. When I went to the store to watch it, so my daddy could go for his afternoon coffee, I told him about the mayor calling out, "Hello, Rudolph Valentino," as I went by and he said I shouldn't be sensi-

tive, that he was just being friendly. Maybe so, but I'm not so sure and I still don't like it. *(Another boy walks by.)*

BOY. Hello, Rudolph Valentino.

HORACE. Hey. *(The boy continues on.)* This Rudolph Valentino business all started, you know, when I won the prize for the best actor at the State Drama Festival. They gave me a medal for being the best actor, but my teacher, Miss Prather, accepted it for the school and it's been two weeks since the Festival and she still hasn't given my medal to me. Miss Prather asked me to meet her after school. She says she has something for me. Maybe it's my medal. Anyway, if that's not what she wants I decided today to ask her for it. I hate doing it, but my mother says she is a busy teacher and has just forgotten she has it, and she won't mind at all my reminding her she has it. I hope she won't. Anyway, I'm going to do it. I want the medal, so I can keep it in my room, and it will be there to remind me of what it was like when I got the medal. Miss Prather said it was very exciting when the three judges called out her name and asked to speak with her and she said she couldn't imagine what they wanted and when she got to them they said is that Robedaux boy playing the drug addict, afflicted or is that acting? And she said, "It's acting." "Very well," they said, "he gets first prize as best actor," and she said she waited around a few minutes longer hoping they were going to say our one act play won the prize for the best play, but when they handed her my medal and said, "Thank you. You may return to your seat now," she knew we hadn't won best play or best production, only best actor. *(A girl walks by.)*

GIRL. Hello, Horace.

HORACE. Hello.

GIRL. Waiting for Miss Prather?

HORACE. Uh-huh.

GIRL. I just saw her in the auditorium.

HORACE. Thanks. *(The girl goes on.)* The next day at school in our speech class she told everybody about my winning best actor, and it was all over school by then anyway and she said in her opinion no one could help being moved at the moment I confessed to my roommates that I was an addict and needed drugs, and then she asked me to wait after class and I did thinking she would give me my medal, but she never mentioned the medal but wanted to know if I was interested in being in the senior play which would start rehearsing in a few weeks. I said I would be and I wanted to tell her I wanted to be an actor, but I didn't know how to. I don't know why I couldn't tell her. Of all the people I know around here she'd likely be the one to understand and encourage me, but I don't know. I just can't bring myself to say out loud: I want to be an actor, not a lawyer or a doctor, an actor. *(A boy walks by.)*

BOY. Hey, Rudolph Valentino.

HORACE. Hey, yourself. *(The boy goes on.)* I've known for a long time too that's what I wanted to be. Since I was thirteen. You see I used to go for walks in the evening with my mother and daddy and we'd always pass on our walks Mr. Armstrong's house. I could always tell when we were approaching his house no matter how dark a night it was, because the fences around his house were covered with honeysuckle vines and you could smell the honeysuckle a block away. Anyway, Mr. Armstrong, a very old man, would always be sitting in the dark on his gallery and as we passed my daddy would always call out, "Good evening, Mr. Armstrong," and he would always answer, "Just fine, thank you. How are you?" even though my daddy had never asked how he was but only wished him a good evening and my daddy explained to me that he always answered that way because he was deaf and couldn't hear what my daddy said, and only imagined what he said and then he would always add, you know Mr. Armstrong was working in the cotton fields in Mississippi when he got a call to come to Texas to preach. And that's what he did. He came here to preach. I had never heard of anyone getting a call before to preach or anything else, so I asked my parents a lot of questions about getting a call. Could anyone get a call? They weren't sure about that since Mr. Armstrong was the only person they ever knew who actually had gotten a call. Was that because he was a Baptist, is that why he got a call? I asked. My mother said no, she had heard about Methodists and Episcopalians getting a call to preach although she hadn't met anyone personally that had except Mr. Armstrong. Anyway, a year later when I turned thirteen I got a call, just as sure as Mr. Armstrong did. Not to preach but to be an actor. I kept that to myself for a month and then I told Jake Lewis, who was my best friend before he had to move away, about it and he said if I wanted his advice I'd keep it to myself as people would think I was peculiar wanting to be something like that. And for good or bad, I've never told anyone else. I asked my mother one time what she thought Mr. Armstrong did when he got his call and she said she couldn't be sure, but she imagined he fell on his knees in the cotton fields and prayed about it and listened to what God wanted him to do and God worked things out for him, so he could come to Texas and preach, and that's what I did, I prayed about it and asked God what I should do and the very next year Miss Prather came here to teach fresh out of college, and she put on plays, and that was encouraging to me and I found out from my daddy where Mr. Dude Arthur's tent show would be in the next few weeks. He always had his itinerary because Mr. Arthur was a customer and often wrote my daddy to send him clothes while he was on the road with his tent show. He asked me why I wanted his address. I said just to write and tell him how much I liked his tent show and he said that was a good idea as Mr. Arthur and his brother Mickey were always very good customers, even though Mr. Arthur was often short on cash and had to have extended credit, since the tent show business was having hard times because of the movies. Anyway, I learned he was going to be in Tyler, Texas in two weeks and I wrote him there, care of general delivery, which is what my father said I should do, and I reminded him in the letter who I was and that I sometimes waited on him in my father's store when he came to Harrison, and I would appreciate it if he wouldn't mention to anyone, not even my daddy, but the next time he was in Harrison, I would like very much him to see him as I wanted to ask him how you go about being an actor. He never answered my letter, so I figured he had never gotten it. So last summer when he came here with his tent show, I went over to the boarding house where he stayed with his wife and Brother Mickey, who plays all the juvenile parts in the tent show, and I told Mr. Arthur I had written him a letter, and had he gotten it. He was drunk and said he didn't remember any letter, what was it about, and I said I wanted advice as I wanted to be an actor. He said why in the name of God, and I said because I wanted to, and I believe I've had a call to be one, and he said, well, you're a fool if you think that and get over it. Mrs. Arthur came in then and said, "Dude, sober up! You have a show tonight," and I left. The next day he came to my daddy's store and in front of me told my daddy that I had come to see him at his boarding house and that I had written him a letter about wanting to be an actor, and after he left my daddy asked was I out of my mind, that being an actor and in a tent show was a terrible way to make a living, that Dude Arthur had told him he was giving up after this season and he was broke, and I said, I guess I shouldn't have, but I did, I said, well, Daddy, that's no worse than being a cotton farmer or a merchant, they are always broke too. But at least, young man, he always calls me young man when he's mad at me, at least young man, I have a roof over my head and I manage to always put food on the table, and I'm not drunk half the time, wondering around the country with only a mortgaged tent to my name. Daddy said he hoped now that this would be the end of such foolishness, and I decided then and there, call or not I would give it up. But when my mother read in the Houston papers that the Ben Greet Players would be in Houston for a week with their Shakespearean repertoire, she said she thought it would be nice for me to go and see them in one of their plays. She wrote my grandmother, my daddy's mother, who lives in Houston and goes to see plays all the time, and she wrote back to send me on to Houston and she would go with me to the play. I went to Houston but she had a headache and couldn't go to the play with me after all. She lived on the street-car line and she said if I went by myself, she would give me real clear directions so I couldn't possibly get lost. So she wrote out for me how to get to the theater and back by the streetcar, and I took the streetcar and I got to the theater just fine, but when I got off the streetcar I saw across the street a sign in front of another theater that read Florence Reed in *The Shanghai Gesture*. I heard my Houston grandmother say that was a wicked play and one that shouldn't be allowed in Houston, and so I don't know what devil got inside me suggesting I go see *The Shanghai Gesture* instead of the Ben Greet Players, but whatever it was, I took my money my mother had given me for the Ben Greet Players and I bought a ticket to see Florence Reed and I guess it was wicked and immoral like my Grandmother in Houston said, but I thought it was wonderful and I said to myself I have to be an actor now somehow, someway. Anyway, I never told my mother or my Houston grandmother I didn't see the Ben Greet Players and when they asked me what play of Shakespeare I had seen, I said, *Julius Caesar* because I had read that play in English class my junior year and I had memorized "Friends, Romans Countrymen, lend me your ears" speech for the class, and I knew if they asked me questions about the play I could answer them. I didn't realize Adelaide Martin, one of my mother's friends, had gone into Houston that same day to see the Ben Greet Players and when she got back she called my mother to tell her about it and my mother said I had been their too, and had liked it a lot and Adelaide said she didn't care for it as she thought the Romeo and Juliet looked middle aged and were too old for their parts. *Romeo and Juliet*, Mama said. "That's not what Horace saw," she said. He saw *Julius Caesar*. "*Julius Caesar*? Did he go to the matinee or the evening

35

show?" Mother said to the matinee and Adelaide said that's the one she attended and there was no *Julius Caesar*, but *Romeo and Juliet*. When I got home from school my mother confronted me with this and I had to admit what I had done. She asked me what the *Shanghai Gesture* was about and I said it took place in a Shanghai Brothel and that's all she had to know. She said I was deceitful and should be ashamed of myself going to a play like that. I guess I should have been, but I wasn't. All I could think about was how Florence Reed reacted when, as the madame of the brothel, heard that her daughter, who she hadn't seen in years, turned up as one of the girls in the brothel. *(A pause. He sings again.)*

"Once I built a railroad,
　Made it run,
　Made it run against time.
　Once I built a railroad,
　Now it's done,
　Brother, can you spare a dime?"

I love to hear Russ Colombo sing that song. My father hates the song. He says its too depressing. He says he likes positive songs like "Happy Days are Here Again." He says the country needs to have songs like that so they'll be in an optimistic mood, and not depressed all the time. *(Two boys come by.)*

1ST BOY. Hey, Horace.

HORACE. Hey.

2ND BOY. What are you hanging around here for?

HORACE. I'm waiting for Miss Prather.

2ND BOY. You have a crush on Miss Prather, don't you?

HORACE. No, I don't have a crush on Miss Prather.

1ST BOY. What are you always hanging around her for?

HORACE. I'm not always hanging around her. I have to see her about something.

1ST BOY. About what?

HORACE. None of your business.

1ST BOY. You're in a good mood today. *(They start out.)*

2ND BOY. *(Calling back.)* Have you decided the college you're going to apply to?

HORACE. No, not yet.

1ST BOY. I'm applying to A & M. *(They continue on.)*

HORACE. Everybody's applying for college that can afford to go. Next time someone asks me about college I think I'll just come right out and say I'm not going to college ever. Not ever. I'm going to be

36

an actor. Yeah. I bet you will. I can't even tell my mother and father. I'm almost scared to, because how my daddy blew up at the store when Dude Arthur told him I wanted to be an actor. I tried last night to tell them. We were sitting together on the porch and there was no moon and it was pitch dark. I could see lightning bugs everywhere and I thought I'll tell them now because it's dark and I don't have to look at their faces when I tell them, but dark or not, I couldn't get the words out. My daddy was going on about the Depression and how hard a time he was having and how bad he felt that he couldn't send me to college this year, and I was saying to myself the whole time. I don't want to go to college, so don't worry about it, but dark or not, I just couldn't get the words out. Mama said, "Are you feeling alright, son? You seem so quiet." "Yes, ma'am," I said, "I feel fine." And my daddy started on about college again and he kept saying over and over he's going to work extra hard at the store in the Fall when the crops come in, and he knows Roosevelt is going to work a miracle and lick the Depression and we'll all have money again like in 1918 and he'll be able to send me to college next fall. "Yes sir," I said. "I appreciate your concern." Then he said, "Well, I'm going to bed. I have to work tomorrow. You better get to bed too, son. You have school tomorrow." "Yes, sir," I said and Mama said kiss me goodnight, son, and I did and went to my room. My daddy and my mother stayed on the porch awhile longer. I undressed and got into bed, but I could hear them talking on the porch and my mother said, "He's so young, hon. If I had to do it over again, I swear I would never have started him in school at five years old. Fifteen is so young to be graduating from high school." "He's not a child, hon," my Father said. "He's a young man. He'll be sixteen by the time he graduates." *(Dorothy Prather, twenty-one, comes in. She has some books and papers and a briefcase.)*

DOROTHY. Forgive me, Horace, for being late. I got detained by an irate mother, who thinks her precious child should've got an A instead of a B. What did you want to see me about?

HORACE. That's alright.

DOROTHY. I wanted to give you a copy of the play I'm doing with you seniors. I want you to read it and tell me how you like it.

HORACE. Thank you. *(She hands him the play.)*

DOROTHY. Its called *Not So Long Ago*. It was done in New York several years ago. Eva Le Gallienne played the lead. She is a very gifted actress. She played in *Lilliom* in New York, you know.

HORACE. Did she?

DOROTHY. Yes. Anyway, that's all I wanted.

HORACE. Yes, ma'am. *(She starts away.)* Miss Prather. I keep meaning to ask you. I never saw the medal I was given for best actor. Do you have it? *(She laughs.)*

DOROTHY. Oh, Horace, I feel terrible. I didn't tell you because I kept hoping it would turn up. I lost your medal.

HORACE. Yes, ma'am.

DOROTHY. I left it at the San Antonio High School after talking to the judges.

HORACE. I see.

DOROTHY. It wasn't until I got back here that I realized what I'd done. I called right away and asked if someone had found it, and they said no, but they'd look out for it and if they found it they would get it to me. Obviously they haven't.

HORACE. Uh-huh.

DOROTHY. You see, when the judges called me up to speak to them about your acting I thought they were calling me to say our play had won first place in the contest and when I realized we hadn't, I was so disappointed I just forgot about your medal. I think I left it on the judges table or somewhere in the auditorium. Anyway, you won and that's what counts. I'm sorry I lost your medal.

HORACE. That's alright. Miss Prather …

DOROTHY. *(Interrupting.)* And Horace, I've been meaning to ask you. Did you ever know any addicts?

HORACE. No, not really. I used to see Miss Sadie Underwood walking past my daddy's store whenever I clerked there on Saturday's and after school. And I heard someone tell my daddy as she walked by that she was addicted to paregoric. My daddy says you can get addicted to Coca-Colas. He says Strachen Newsome was addicted to Coca-Colas, drank nine or ten a day until they ate the lining of his stomach and he died from drinking too many Coca-Colas.

DOROTHY. My heavens. Well. Nice to see you, Horace. Read the play and tell me what you think.

HORACE. Yes, ma'am. *(She starts away.)* Miss Prather?

DOROTHY. Yes.

HORACE. I haven't told my mother and daddy about this yet, so please don't say anything about it to anyone. *(A pause.)* My daddy can't afford to send me to college next year.

DOROTHY. I'm sorry, Horace.

HORACE. That's alright, but he says he hopes to be able to send me the following year.

DOROTHY. A year will go quickly, you know.

HORACE. Yes, ma'am, but I don't want to go to college.

DOROTHY. Never?

HORACE. Never.

DOROTHY. Oh, Horace.

HORACE. Never.

DOROTHY. Why, Horace?

HORACE. Well, *(A pause. Then almost blurting out:)* I want to be an actor.

DOROTHY. Oh, well.

HORACE. I've heard there are acting schools.

DOROTHY. Yes, there are.

HORACE. Do you know about acting schools?

DOROTHY. A little. How do your parents feel about this?

HORACE. I don't know. I haven't told them.

DOROTHY. I think you should tell them, Horace.

HORACE. I'm going to. I read in *The Chronicle* the other day that someone from Houston was studying acting in Pasadena, California.

DOROTHY. Yes, there is a school there. At the Pasadena Playhouse. They have summer courses, and as a matter of fact I was thinking of taking some courses this summer and I thought it might be interesting to go to an acting school that had a summer course. Pasadena was one and I was considering the American Academy as the other.

HORACE. Where is that?

DOROTHY. In New York City.

HORACE. Oh. Are they expensive, Miss Prather?

DOROTHY. They're not cheap. I have catalogues from both of them. Would you like to take them home and look them over? *(She opens a briefcase.)* I have them here. *(She hands them to Horace.)*

HORACE. Thank you so much.

DOROTHY. You're welcome, Horace. Think carefully about all of this, Horace. You are talented certainly, but you are so very young.

HORACE. Yes, ma'am. *(A section of the living room of the Robedaux house. There is an upright piano here and several chairs. Elizabeth, thirty-five, Horace's mother, is there playing "Narcissus" on the piano. Jim, Horace's younger brother, nine, enters.)*

JIM. Ma, can I go to the movies this afternoon? *(She continues playing, not paying any attention to him. He walks over to her and says in a very loud voice, making himself heard over the piano, "Ma, can I go to the movies tonight? I've done all my homework." Elizabeth stops playing and looks at him.)*

ELIZABETH. May I go to the movies tonight?

JIM. May I? I've done all of my homework.

ELIZABETH. All of it?

JIM. Every single bit of it.

ELIZABETH. What's playing?

JIM. I don't know. It's a talking picture, I know that much.

ELIZABETH. Aren't they all talking pictures these days?

JIM. No, ma'am. Some are just part talking and on Saturdays the serials are all silent.

ELIZABETH. Well, call the theater and see what's playing.

JIM. I've done all my homework.

ELIZABETH. That's all well and good, but I still don't want you to go and see just any talking picture. Some pictures are not suitable, in my opinion, for children. *(He goes. She continues playing "Narcissus." Jim comes in.)*

JIM. Mama. *(She continues playing.)* Mama?

ELIZABETH. *(As she continues playing.)* Yes?

JIM. I know the name of the picture.

ELIZABETH. *(She continues playing.)* What?

JIM. *Weary River.*

ELIZABETH. *Weary River?* What's that about?

JIM. I don't know. They said it was a love story.

ELIZABETH. A what?

JIM. A love story.

ELIZABETH. Did they say it was suitable for children?

JIM. I don't know. I didn't ask.

ELIZABETH. Who's in it?

JIM. Lila Lee, Betty Compson and Richard Barthelmes.

ELIZABETH. I don't think so.

JIM. Mom.

ELIZABETH. No, Jim. It all sounds too adult to me. Anyway, movies are expensive. You just can't go to the movies every time you turn around.

JIM. You let Horace go to the tent show every night when it's in town.

ELIZABETH. But that's only for a week. Anyway, Mr. Dude Arthur always trades at your daddy's store while he's in town. You could go to the tent show every night if you wanted to.

JIM. I don't like tent shows. I like the movies. The movies only cost a dime for children.

ELIZABETH. Only a dime. Dimes don't grow on trees, you know. *(Horace enters. He has schoolbooks.)* Hello, son.

HORACE. Hello.

ELIZABETH. How was school?

HORACE. OK. Miss Prather gave me a copy of the senior play she's doing.

JIM. Are you going to be in it?

HORACE. Yes.

JIM. Are you going to play the lead?

HORACE. I don't know.

JIM. I bet you do. All the kids say Miss Prather thinks you hung the moon.

HORACE. I'm going to go read the play.

ELIZABETH. Do you have homework?

HORACE. Not much. *(He goes. She continues playing.)*

JIM. I wonder if this one is going to be about a dope fiend too. Kids that saw the play in San Antonio said when he told his roommates he was a dope fiend and needed dope right at that moment he began to tremble and shake. They thought he was going to have a fit. I wish I could have seen it. *(Horace, Sr. comes in.)*

HORACE, SR. Hello.

ELIZABETH. You're early.

HORACE, SR. I know. *(He kisses her on the cheek.)* Run on, Jim.

JIM. Why?

HORACE, SR. I want to talk to your mother about something.

JIM. About what?

HORACE, SR. Never mind about what. Just leave us alone for a while. *(He goes.)* Where's Horace?

ELIZABETH. He's in his room.

HORACE, SR. Studying?

ELIZABETH. I don't think so. Miss Prather gave him a copy today of the play they're doing as the Senior Play.

HORACE, SR. Elizabeth, as you know, I've always felt leaving school as I had to do in the sixth grade in order to go to work to support myself was a great disadvantage to me. I've always felt if I had only had a proper education, finished high school, gone to college. *(A pause.)* Well, I wouldn't always feel such a terrible failure. I haven't accomplished much, you know.

ELIZABETH. I don't agree. I think on the contrary you have

41

managed very well in these terrible times. We have all the food we need, we have the clothes we need, and we have this house.

HORACE, SR. Which your papa gave us.

ELIZABETH. Never mind. We've never had to mortgage it. We …

HORACE, SR. I get no credit for that. I couldn't mortgage it even if I wanted to. You are not allowed to mortgage your homestead in the state of Texas. It's against the law. Anyway, it's not about me. It's about Horace, Jr. I've been thinking more and more this last week about his graduation. Do you realize he'll be graduating in two months?

ELIZABETH. I know. Is it possible?

HORACE, SR. I was thinking all day yesterday and last night and again today, what would I most want to change about my life? And, of course, I would like to have been able to finish high school and go to college and get a profession like law or medicine, or engineering, but I was never good in math, so I probably couldn't have been an engineer. Anyway, something to give me a proper education so I'd be equipped to do more than run a store. All that's too late for me now, of course, but I remember so well when Horace, Jr. was born I made a promise to myself I was going to see when he grew up he was going to have all the advantages my mama couldn't give me. I thought today that's all well and good to remember promises, but what can I do about the promises? I can barely keep the store afloat these days, as you know. I've had to go to the bank twice and borrow money to pay current bills. I tell you I felt so sad and blue, and I thought where in the world can I turn now. When Mr. Beard came into the store I thought it's not the first of the month, why is he here to pay his rent? And so I said you're early. Your rent's not due for another week. And then I thought to myself something about the house needs fixing and he's here to get me to have it done and I asked him if that's why he was here, or was he here to pay his rent early. "No," he said, "I'm not here for either reason, but to talk to you about some business." "What kind of business," I said. "Have you ever thought about selling your rent house?" he asked. "No, I haven't," I said. "You bought it from your father-in-law, didn't you," he said. "Yes," I said, "in 1918. Cotton was selling for forty cents a pound and the war was on and everybody had a little money then." "Do you remember what you paid for it?" "Yes." "Well, would you be willing to sell it to me now if you made a profit?" "Well, I'd certainly think about it. I have to talk it over with my wife first, of course." "I understand," he said.

"I'll pay you three thousand dollars for the house." "Yes, sir," I said. "Let me talk to my wife." And that's a thousand-dollar profit, you know, hon. And I figure the three thousand dollars will get Horace, Jr. into not a fancy college maybe, but a good one and it will see him through four years. Of course, he won't be able to join a fraternity and he'll have to come back here and work with me in the store during summer vacations. *(A pause.)* What do you think?

ELIZABETH. Well …

HORACE, SR. I think it's a miracle, honey. The rent house is old and needs repairs. I've never been able to rent it for more than twenty dollars a month and …

ELIZABETH. Well, it's certainly alright with me. I'm sure Horace, Jr. will just be delighted.

HORACE, SR. Without saying anything about it, I've been sending off for catalogues of schools I knew were reasonable. I have some down at the store he can look at tonight. *(Jim enters.)* Where's Horace?

JIM. He's in his room.

ELIZABETH. What's he doing?

JIM. He's muttering to himself. I think he's reading aloud about that play they're doing.

HORACE, SR. Go tell him to come here.

JIM. Yes, sir. *(He goes.)*

HORACE, SR. Shall I tell him or you?

ELIZABETH. You tell him. *(Horace enters.)*

HORACE, SR. Horace?

HORACE. Yes, sir.

HORACE, SR. Sit down, son.

HORACE. Yes, sir. *(A pause.)*

HORACE, SR. Son, you know our rent house the Beards are renting?

HORACE. Yes, sir.

HORACE, SR. I'm going to sell it.

HORACE. To whom?

HORACE, SR. Mr. Beard. He came to the store today and offered to buy it.

HORACE. Do you want to sell it, Daddy?

HORACE, SR. Yes, I do. It's rundown, you know, and I'll never be able to get much rent the state it's in. *(A pause.)* You know why I'm so happy I can sell it?

HORACE. No, sir.

HORACE, SR. So I can do for you what my mama couldn't ever do for me.

HORACE. What's that, Daddy?

HORACE, SR. Send you to college. Of course, it will have to be a state school. And you won't be able to join a fraternity or anything fancy like that. I have been figuring ever since talking to Mr. Beard and I can just about manage four years for what I'll get for the house.

HORACE. What are you selling it for?

HORACE, SR. Three thousand dollars.

ELIZABETH. Isn't it wonderful, Horace?

HORACE. Yes, ma'am.

HORACE, SR. And I have a lot of college catalogues at the store we could look over together and after supper I'll go down and get them and bring them back here.

HORACE. Yes, sir. *(Horace, Sr. looks at his watch.)*

HORACE, SR. What time is supper, Elizabeth?

ELIZABETH. In another hour.

HORACE, SR. I tell you what. I think I'll go down now and get those catalogues and we can begin looking at them before supper.

HORACE. Yes, sir. *(A pause.)* Daddy?

HORACE, SR. Yes, son.

HORACE. I feel terrible about this, but I have to tell you something.

HORACE, SR. Tell me what, Son?

HORACE. I don't want to go to college.

HORACE, SR. What?

HORACE. I don't want to go to college.

HORACE, SR. You have to go to college, son. You'll regret it the rest of your life if you don't go to college. If you go to college you'll have all kinds of opportunities I never had. I want you to go to college.

HORACE. I don't want to go to college, Dad.

ELIZABETH. Why not, son?

HORACE. I don't know how to tell you, but I just don't.

HORACE, SR. You can tell me, son. I'm your father. Don't be afraid. I'll understand. Whatever it is.

HORACE. Yes, sir. I hope so. *(A pause.)* I don't want to go to college, because I want to be an actor and …

HORACE, SR. Good God Almighty! Did you hear that, Elizabeth? Am I dreaming, or did he say what I think he did? What did he say, Elizabeth?

ELIZABETH. You heard him correctly. He said he doesn't want to go to college, because he wants to be an actor.

HORACE, SR. An actor! An actor! What kind of an actor? Like Wallace Reid who died a dope fiend? Like Fatty Arbunkle arrested in a sex scandal? Like Charlie Chaplain seducing young innocent girls? Or maybe like Dude Arthur, with his tent show, half-drunk all the time. Talk to him about the life of an actor. You know what he told me? He said he'd rather a child of his would take a pistol and blow his brains out than be an actor.

ELIZABETH. Come on, honey. Just calm down now.

HORACE, SR. Where do such ideas come from? Where did he get such an idea here in Harrison, Texas? Did your teacher put all this in your head? Has she put you up to all this? What is the new play you're in about? More dope fiends?

HORACE. No, sir. It's a period piece about life in New York City. Eva Le Gallienne played in it in New York.

HORACE, SR. Who in the world is that?

HORACE. I don't really know, sir. I only know what Miss Prather told me. She said she is a great actress. She was in *Lilliom* in New York City.

HORACE, SR. In what?

HORACE. *Lilliom.*

HORACE, SR. What's that?

HORACE. What's what?

HORACE, SR. *Lilliom* or whatever you said.

HORACE. That was a play in New York.

HORACE, SR. Is that about dope, too?

HORACE. No, sir. I don't think so. I don't know what it's about.

HORACE, SR. Well, where did all this foolishness come from if not from that teacher of yours?

HORACE. Do you remember old Mr. Armstrong?

HORACE, SR. Yes.

HORACE. And you used to tell me he had a call to come to Texas to preach?

HORACE, SR. Yes.

HORACE. Well, one day I had a call just —

HORACE, SR. *(Interrupting.)* You had a what?

HORACE. A call.

HORACE, SR. What kind of a call?

HORACE. It's hard to describe, Daddy. It's just like something came to me and said you want to be an actor.

HORACE, SR. I never heard of such thing. Did it say aloud, "You want to be an actor?"

HORACE. No, sir. Not really, but I heard it.

HORACE, SR. I understand you heard it, but was it a man's voice or a woman's voice?

HORACE. No, sir. Come to think of it. It was more like a feeling, like …

HORACE, SR. Like what?

HORACE. I don't know, sir. It was like nothing I have ever experienced before, or since.

HORACE, SR. God Almighty. I never heard of such a thing. *(A pause.)* Well, what did you do after this whatever it was spoke to you?

HORACE. I went to Mother and I asked what Mr. Armstrong did after he got his call, and Mother said he probably prayed and asked God to tell him what to do. So I prayed and asked God to tell me what to do.

HORACE, SR. How long ago was this?

HORACE. About a year and a half ago.

HORACE, SR. Why didn't you tell your mother and me about it?

HORACE. I thought you'd make fun of me, and tell me I was foolish and crazy. Then soon after Miss Prather came here to teach and began to put on plays, and I thought maybe God sent her to help me be an actor, and I prayed some more.

ELIZABETH. How did you pray, Son?

HORACE. I just prayed. I prayed to know if I should tell Miss Prather that I wanted to be an actor. But I was afraid to just then, so I didn't. But it came to me to write Mr. Dude Arthur to see if I could see him next time he was in Harrison and ask him how I could go about being an actor. I wrote him, but he never answered. The next time his show was in town I went by his boarding house and he was there, but he was drunk. I decided not to ask him anything then and started to leave, but he kept asking me why I had come there. I finally said I had written him a letter and sent it to Tyler, Texas and had he gotten it. He said no and what was the letter about. I said I wanted advice on how to become an actor. He said why in the name of God. I said because I wanted to know as I wanted to spend my life when I got out of high school acting. He said, well, you're a fool and get over it. Mrs. Arthur came in then and she yelled at him and said he'd better start sobering up as he had a show that night. I left and the next day while he was at the store with Daddy, he came in and he told Daddy about my visit to him and that I said I wanted to be an actor. After he left Daddy yelled at me and said he'd never heard of such a thing and to get over it.

ELIZABETH. Is that right, Horace?

HORACE, SR. Yes, it is.

ELIZABETH. You never told me about it.

HORACE, SR. I didn't see any use in worrying you, as I knew he'd get over it. You remember George Rust said he wanted to be a painter, and his family sent him East to study and after two years he came back here and built him a studio, so he could spend his time painting and it lasted about six months and then he got tired of it so he ended up managing his family's cotton farm.

HORACE. Anyway, since Daddy was so opposed to it and Mr. Arthur wasn't at all encouraging, I decided maybe God hadn't spoken to me after all, and I wasn't going to be an actor. But then Mother asked if I wanted to go and see the Ben Greet Players. I said, yes, and when I got to the theater where they were playing, I looked across the street where Florence Reed was playing and something told me to go there instead of to the Ben Greet Players. So I went to that instead of the Ben Greet Players and when the play was over I knew I had to be an actor for sure now and I told Miss Prather what I wanted to do today. She wasn't as encouraging as I thought she would surely be, but she said if that's what I wanted to do, I should go to school.

ELIZABETH. What kind of school, honey?

HORACE. A theater school where they teach acting.

ELIZABETH. Are there such things? I didn't know that.

HORACE. Yes, ma'am. And she had sent away for catalogues for a school in Pasadena and in New York City, which is the one I like the best.

ELIZABETH. Why, honey?

HORACE. Because that's where Broadway is and they have lots of theaters there and …

HORACE, SR. (*Interrupting.*) Well, I'll tell you this. As sure as I'm standing here, you'll get over it. Mr. Armstrong got over his call. He only preached for five years and when he saw he couldn't half feed his family on a preacher's salary, he began to sell insurance. (*A pause.*)

HORACE. Dad?

HORACE, SR. Yes?

HORACE. I have some catalogues in my room from acting schools. Would you look at them?

HORACE, SR. No. It's all a lot of foolishness.

47

HORACE. Daddy?

HORACE, SR. Yes?

HORACE. Help me, Daddy. I'll never ask you for anything again in my life, but just help me and send me someplace where I can learn to be an actor. I'll never ask you for anything else ever again. I swear. *(He begins to cry.)* I swear. I know it's crazy, Daddy. I don't expect you and Mother to understand, but ... *(He's sobbing now. He controls himself.)* I'm sorry. I'm sorry. *(He leaves his parents disturbed and troubled by his crying. There is silence for a moment.)*

HORACE, SR. Well ... *(Jim comes in.)*

JIM. What's the matter with Horace?

ELIZABETH. Never mind. We'll talk about it later.

JIM. He was crying.

ELIZABETH. We're aware of it.

JIM. I never saw him cry before. He's sixteen. He shouldn't be crying at sixteen.

ELIZABETH. He's not sixteen yet.

JIM. He will be in March.

ELIZABETH. It isn't March yet.

HORACE, SR. Go ask Horace, Jr. to give you the catalogues of the schools he was telling me about, and bring them to me.

JIM. What schools?

HORACE, SR. I don't know the names of them. He'll know what I'm talking about. *(Jim goes.)* When I was in the bank I saw Louie Worthing. He's prospered, you know.

ELIZABETH. I know he has.

HORACE, SR. Made good investments.

ELIZABETH. I know.

HORACE, SR. He said he was investing in an oil pool, and that there was just one share left, and he didn't want to influence me one way or the other, but he's investing in the oil pool, and he thinks whoever invests in the pool can make quite a profit from their investment.

ELIZABETH. How much does the share cost?

HORACE, SR. Three thousand dollars, and I was tempted to invest the money I will get from Mr. Beard, but I said to myself, if I lose the money, there goes Horace's college money. *(Jim comes in with two catalogues. Horace, Sr. takes the catalogues and looks at them. Jim goes to the radio, turns it on and looks for a program with music. The phone rings in another part of the house. Horace, Sr. goes to answer it. Jim finds a station with popular music.)*

ELIZABETH. Would you mind not playing that music now, Jim? *(He looks around at her.)* Just turn the radio off, please, Jim?

JIM. Why is everybody so upset? *(Horace, Sr. comes back in and picks up the catalogues he had been looking at.)*

ELIZABETH. Who was on the phone?

HORACE, SR. Louie Worthing. He says there is someone interested in that last share in the oil pool. He will have to give them an answer by nine tonight. He said he wanted me to understand he's putting no pressure on me, but he just thought I should know and I would have to decide before nine tonight. *(He looks at his watch.)*

ELIZABETH. What time is it, Horace?

HORACE, SR. Seven. *(A pause.)* Of course, if Horace refuses to go to college I don't need the three thousand dollars right now. And if they strike oil as Louie believes they will, our whole life could turn around. What should I do, Elizabeth?

ELIZABETH. I don't know.

HORACE, SR. Of course I won't need money for Jim's college for another seven years. That is if he wants to go to college. *(To Jim.)* I hope you don't wind up wanting to be an actor like your brother.

JIM. No, sir. I'd like to be a crooner, but I know I can't be, because I can't carry a tune unless I'm singing along with somebody.

HORACE, SR. Thank God for small favors. *(A pause.)* I'm going to call Louie and tell him he can count me in on the pool. *(He starts out of the room. He stops, thinking for a beat. He comes back into the room.)* I can't do it. As sure as I invest in that oil well and lose my money, Horace will come to me and say I've changed my mind and I want to go to college. *(A pause. He picks up the catalogues and looks at them.)*

JIM. Horace told me just now he'll never go to college. That he's going to be an actor. He says he had a call.

HORACE, SR. I know all about that call business.

ELIZABETH. If he goes to acting school, Pasadena is cheaper than New York.

HORACE, SR. I'll never help him to get to New York to school. Not a fifteen-year-old boy.

JIM. He's almost sixteen.

HORACE, SR. You keep out of it, Jim. How much is Pasadena?

ELIZABETH. It's a two-year course. Seven hundred and fifty dollars for the first year and two hundred and fifty dollars for the second. Mama has two sisters out in California. Aunt Mag and Aunt Bobo.

HORACE, SR. I remember.

ELIZABETH. A thousand dollars for two years. That will still leave you two thousand dollars.

HORACE, SR. Not really. Does the two thousand include board and room?

ELIZABETH. No, I guess not.

HORACE, SR. And there is the fare to California and back.

ELIZABETH. He could take the bus.

HORACE, SR. Even the bus costs money, Elizabeth. You see it all adds up. *(A pause.)* And what worries me the most is does a fifteen-year-old boy really know what he wants to do? What if we send him out there and he doesn't like it and wants to go to college? What then?

ELIZABETH. I don't know what then. I'm no fortune-teller. *(A pause.)* He was very upset, I only know that. I've never seen him so upset. Have you?

HORACE, SR. No. *(A pause.)* Here's what I think we should do. Make a bargain with him. Let him stay here next year after he graduates and work with me in the store, and if at the end of the year he still wants to go to acting school, we'll send him to Pasadena. Does that seem sensible to you?

ELIZABETH. Yes, it does. It sounds very sensible to me.

HORACE, SR. Of course, I think he'll change his mind while he waits out the year. He'll realize how chancy this whole acting business is and comes to his senses and say I was wrong, I want to go to college. In the meantime I'll leave all the college catalogues I sent for around the living room so he can see them and look at them if he wants to. *(Calling.)* Horace, Jr.

HORACE. *(Calling offstage.)* Yes, sir.

HORACE, SR. Can you come here please? *(Horace, Sr. goes back to looking at the catalogues he has. Horace, Jr. enters.)*

HORACE. Yes, sir.

HORACE, SR. Sit down, son.

HORACE. Yes, sir.

HORACE, SR. We've been looking over the catalogues.

HORACE. Yes, sir.

HORACE, SR. Does either of these schools guarantee you a job when you finish their curriculum?

HORACE. I don't believe so, sir.

JIM. No college guarantees you a job, Daddy.

HORACE, SR. You keep out of this, Jim, or I'll send you to your room.

JIM. Yes, sir.

HORACE, SR. You see, I don't want you to think your daddy doesn't want to help you in anyway. I can, but we just want to be sure it's what you really want to do.

HORACE. I understand, Papa.

HORACE, SR. You know Mr. George Rust?

HORACE. Yes, sir.

HORACE, SR. Well, when he was seventeen and graduated from high school he said he wanted to be a painter.

JIM. What kind of painter? A house painter?

HORACE. No, not a house painter, Jim. An artist. He wanted to paint pictures of people and houses and cotton fields and God knows what all. That's all he would do from morning until night, and he got his family to send him East so he could study painting and off he went and stayed away for two years and studied painting and came back here and his family built him a studio and he painted night and day and then he got tired of it and quit and he's never painted a day since and manages his family's cotton farm.

HORACE. You told me about that earlier, Daddy.

HORACE, SR. Oh, did I? I guess I did.

ELIZABETH. And I had a cousin in Brazoria who was bound and determined to be an artist of some kind, and her family sent her to live in Greenwich Village where she could be an artist. She even got into O.O. McIntyre's column in New York about something she did in Greenwich Village like squirting some red ink on the monument in Washington Square, or something like that, and then she lost her mind, the poor thing, and they had to bring her back home and she wound up in the asylum.

HORACE. I'm not going to lose my mind, Mama. I'm going to work hard and made a success.

ELIZABETH. I'm sure you will, darling, but I just want you to know why we worry.

HORACE, SR. *(Glancing at the Playhouse brochure.)* Who is Gilmore Brown?

HORACE. It says there, he's the head of the Playhouse. The artistic director.

HORACE, SR. I see. And who is Charles Prickett?

HORACE. According to the brochure he's the business manager. *(A pause.)*

HORACE, SR. Well, I'll make a bargain with you. Wait a year until you're seventeen and work in the store with me in the meantime. If at the end of the year you still want to study acting, I'll help you go to Pasadena. *(Horace is moved and relieved by their decision, but controls his emotions.)*

HORACE. Yes, sir. Thank you, sir. I appreciate it. *(He goes.)*

HORACE, SR. Well, I bet you anything I have he'll come to his senses after a month or two here working in the store and he'll say I've changed my mind. I want to go to college. *(A pause.)* Do I have time to work in the garden a little before supper?

ELIZABETH. Yes, you do.

JIM. What are we having?

ELIZABETH. Nothing special. A casserole. Horace, what if he doesn't change his mind?

HORACE, SR. Then I don't know. *(He goes.)*

ELIZABETH. Jim, in about half an hour set the table for me, will you?

JIM. Yes, ma'am. *(She goes. He picks up the Pasadena brochure and looks at it. Horace comes in.)* Who are Onshlow Stevens and Gloria Stewart?

HORACE. Why?

JIM. It says here they are movie stars and went to the Pasadena Playhouse and were discovered there by Hollywood. Did you ever hear of them?

HORACE. Yes, I did.

JIM. Well I haven't. And Victor Jory. Did you ever hear of him?

HORACE. Yes, I did.

JIM. Are you calmer now?

HORACE. Yes, I am. *(Elizabeth enters. Horace takes the Pasadena brochure and starts to look at it. He begins to sing to himself.)*

"Once I built a railroad,
  Made it run,
  Made it run against time.
  Once I built a railroad,
  Now it's done,
  Brother, can you spare a dime?"

ELIZABETH. Horace?

HORACE. Yes, ma'am.

ELIZABETH. Would you mind not singing that song around your father? He finds it depressing.

HORACE. Yes, ma'am. *(He puts the brochure down. Jim picks it up and begins reading it. Elizabeth takes the American Academy brochure and begins to read that. Horace walks to the front of the stage and addresses the audience.)* My father asked me not to tell anyone in town that he was thinking of sending me to dramatic school until it was time for me to go. Jim said he kept hoping I'd change my mind and ask to go to college. At first he left college catalogues all over the house. But when he saw I wasn't going to change my mind they began to disappear. A lot of my friends went off to college, those that didn't, mostly went to Houston looking for jobs. Dude Arthur's tent show came for one last summer and then it closed down for good. They did a show in Harrison called a "Womanless Wedding" with men from town playing all the parts. "Dearie" Burtner, who was big and fat and had been my Scout Master when I was in Cub Scouts was the bride and Mr. Piney, who was thin as a rake and only came up to Dearie's shoulders was the groom. They asked me to be in it, but I declined. People in town said that was the kind of show they liked. Clean, wholesome and fun. Vilma Hanky and Rod LaRocque, two movie stars that couldn't get work because of their accents when talkies began, came to Houston in a play called *Cherries are Ripe*. I went to see it, but I didn't like it. The well Louie Worthing's pool invested in came through and Louie Worthing and all his investors became rich. Some said they made as much as fifty thousand apiece. Anyway, the ones I knew all got new cars for themselves and their wives and children. It wasn't until years later my mother told me Daddy could have been one of the investors, but was afraid they would find no oil and the three thousand dollars he had for me would be lost. When news got around town that my folks were sending me off to dramatic school, my daddy had many visitors. Mostly old men, he said, came to the store to tell him he was making a mistake and just throwing his money away. Most of them he said used George Rust as an example of how it would finally turn out. I was in the store when the last one came in. An uncle on Daddy's side. I was in the front of the store and Daddy was in the back at his desk working on his accounts when this uncle came in. He barely spoke to me and asked where Daddy was and I pointed to the back of the store, and I called out, "Daddy, Uncle Albert is here to see you." He went on towards Daddy in the back of the store. I could hear him say he was here as a concerned member of the family to try and talk some sense into Daddy. I heard Daddy say he would thank him to mind his own business. Then his uncle brought up George Rust one more time and they began to yell at each other over that and his uncle left in a fury without saying goodbye to Daddy or me. The night I was to leave for California he and Mother went to sit on the gallery after supper. I was in my room packing my suitcase while listening to the radio, when Daddy called and asked me to come out on the porch. I went out and there was a moon, partly obscured by a cloud, but high in the sky. Daddy gave me my bus ticket and told me to be careful of pickpockets, and I said I would. He gave me a twenty dollar bill then, which he said I should save in case of an emergency of some kind came up. I thanked him and Mother began crying then and said they were going to miss me. I said I would miss them too. Daddy said they were both very proud of me and felt I would have a wonderful success, but to always remember that if things didn't work out in California or any other place, I could always come back to my home and be welcomed and there would be a place for me to work in his store. I thanked him for telling me that. I never did go back during their lifetime except on visits, though many a time when I was lonely and discouraged I wanted to. But then I remembered about my call and kept on going somehow. *(The lights fade.)*

End of Play

PROPERTY LIST

Books
Script
Briefcase
Brochures

SOUND EFFECTS

"Narcissus" played on the piano
Radio
Phone rings

NEW PLAYS

★ **AUGUST: OSAGE COUNTY by Tracy Letts.** WINNER OF THE 2008 PULITZER PRIZE AND TONY AWARD. When the large Weston family reunites after Dad disappears, their Oklahoma homestead explodes in a maelstrom of repressed truths and unsettling secrets. "Fiercely funny and bitingly sad." *–NY Times.* "Ferociously entertaining." *–Variety.* "A hugely ambitious, highly combustible saga." *–NY Daily News.* [6M, 7W] ISBN: 978-0-8222-2300-9

★ **RUINED by Lynn Nottage.** WINNER OF THE 2009 PULITZER PRIZE. Set in a small mining town in Democratic Republic of Congo, RUINED is a haunting, probing work about the resilience of the human spirit during times of war. "A full-immersion drama of shocking complexity and moral ambiguity." *–Variety.* "Sincere, passionate, courageous." *–Chicago Tribune.* [8M, 4W] ISBN: 978-0-8222-2390-0

★ **GOD OF CARNAGE by Yasmina Reza, translated by Christopher Hampton.** WINNER OF THE 2009 TONY AWARD. A playground altercation between boys brings together their Brooklyn parents, leaving the couples in tatters as the rum flows and tensions explode. "Satisfyingly primitive entertainment." *–NY Times.* "Elegant, acerbic, entertainingly fueled on pure bile." *–Variety.* [2M, 2W] ISBN: 978-0-8222-2399-3

★ **THE SEAFARER by Conor McPherson.** Sharky has returned to Dublin to look after his irascible, aging brother. Old drinking buddies Ivan and Nicky are holed up at the house too, hoping to play some cards. But with the arrival of a stranger from the distant past, the stakes are raised ever higher. "Dark and enthralling Christmas fable." *–NY Times.* "A timeless classic." *–Hollywood Reporter.* [5M] ISBN: 978-0-8222-2284-2

★ **THE NEW CENTURY by Paul Rudnick.** When the playwright is Paul Rudnick, expectations are geared for a play both hilarious and smart, and this provocative and outrageous comedy is no exception. "The one-liners fly like rockets." *–NY Times.* "The funniest playwright around." *–Journal News.* [2M, 3W] ISBN: 978-0-8222-2315-3

★ **SHIPWRECKED! AN ENTERTAINMENT—THE AMAZING ADVENTURES OF LOUIS DE ROUGEMONT (AS TOLD BY HIMSELF) by Donald Margulies.** The amazing story of bravery, survival and celebrity that left nineteenth-century England spellbound. Dare to be whisked away. "A deft, literate narrative." *–LA Times.* "Springs to life like a theatrical pop-up book." *–NY Times.* [2M, 1W] ISBN: 978-0-8222-2341-2

DRAMATISTS PLAY SERVICE, INC.
440 Park Avenue South, New York, NY 10016 212-683-8960 Fax 212-213-1539
postmaster@dramatists.com www.dramatists.com